93 of the best Housewives quotes from around the world

TERENCE WEBB

Kyle Richards:

"You're such a f---ing liar, Camille!"

NeNe Leakes to Kenya Moore:

"So nasty and so rude."

Ramona Singer to Aviva Drescher:

"Take a Xanax! Calm Down!

Teresa Giudice to Danielle Staub:

"Prostitution whore!"

Camille Grammer:

"The morally corrupt Faye Resnick."

Vicki Gunvalson:

"When do you send a little family van for six people?!"

Sheree Whitfield to party planner:

"Who gon' check me, boo?"

Kelly to Ramona Singer:

"Your blood type is pinot grigio."

Tamra Judge to Alexis Bellino:

"You are psychotic, Jesus Jugs!"

Kim Richards to Brandi Glanville:

"You're a slut pig!"

Caroline Manzo to Danielle Staub:

"Let me tell you something about my family. We're as thick as thieves and we protect each other 'til the end."

NeNe Leakes to Kim Zolciak-Biermann:

"Close your legs to married men."

Countess Luann de Lesseps to Heather Thomson:

"Don't be all, like, uncool."

Lisa Vanderpump:

"Checkmate, bitch."

Phaedra Parks to Kenya Moore:

"You can't be a Housewife because you don't have a husband."

Kim Zolciak-Biermann:

"Dear God, please keep my wig on."

Kenya Moore:

"I'm gone with the wind fabulous!"

Taylor Armstrong:

"I'm about to take you out back and pull some Oklahoma on your ass."

Dina Manzo on Danielle Staub:

"This girl is obsessed with me, I don't know if she wants to be me, or skin me and wear me like last year's Versace..."

Luann de Lesseps to Alex McCord:

"And you came in, in your Herman Munster shoes."

Candiace Dillard: "I invited her into my home. I gave her a beverage."

Luann de Lesseps & Bethenny Frankel:

"Please don't let it be about Tom." "It's about Tom."

Karen Huger:

"People come for me all the time, they just don't find me."

Dorinda Medley:

"I decorated! I cooked! I made it nice!"

Denise Richards:

"I'm F***Ing Denise Richards, Kyle"

Lisa Vanderpump:

"I haven't ridden anything this big in ages"

Aviva Drescher:

"The only thing artificial or fake about me.....
IS THIS!"

Dana Wilkey:

"Did you know? $25,000."

Ken Todd:

"Goodbye, Kyle!"

Vicki Gunvalson:

"We're going to get Gretchen wasted. Naked wasted."

Erika Girardi:

"They're Not Paying My Bills. So Why Would I Really Give A FUCK About What They Think?"

Shannon Beador:

"This isn't my plate you fucking bitch"

Dorinda Medley:

"I'll tell you how I'm doing...not well, bitch"

Heather Dubrow:

"If everyone says you're dead, it's time to lie down!"

Dorit Kemsley:

"My mothers best friend is black"

Nene Leakes:

"Bye Wig"

Aviva Drescher:

"You're both white trash, quite frankly"

Yolanda Hadid:

"Who is Adrienne Maloof in this world"

Camille Grammer:

"But now we said it"

Erika Girardi:

"You don't know what I go through at night"

Brandi Redmond:

"She should just steal the money like I do. I just take it out of his wallet"

Lisa Rinna:

"Were people doing coke in your bathroom?"

Brandi Glanville:

"At least I don't do crystal meth in the bathroom all night long, bitch"

Carole Radziwill:

"I was awoken in the night by two male voices. One was Luanns"

Margaret Josephs:

"Your husbands in the pool"

Bethenny Frankel:

"I would blow Simon Van Kempen for a slurpee right now."

Mary Cosby:

"You smell like hospital"

Meredith Marks:

"Thank You, I'm Disengaging. I Am Not Engaging"

Jen Shah:

"You're Gonna Go With Mary, Who F***Ed Her Grandfather?"

Athena X:

"When you lie with animals, you become an animal"

Louise Wallace:

"I made my money the old fashioned way, I inherited it"

Mary Cosby:

"Can you get the airpods? I want them back"

Lydia Schiavello:

"The restaurant was on the seventy-oneth floor"

Kim Richards:

"You're a slut pig"

Gizelle Bryant:

"I am not participating"

Brandi Redmond:

"My hat is beautiful, it has green moss, little brown rabbit turds and a toilet seat, poop and a dog on it"

Stephanie Hollman:

"Travis gives me a list of chores. It's kind of my way to make my money in the marriage"

Leanne Locken:

"She's gonna come for me one day and it isn't going to be pretty. Her husband gets his dick sucked at The Round-Up. I know the boys who did it"

Robyn Dixon:

"I am so glad Juan Dixon is not here right now"

Gizelle Bryant:

"I have a legacy and a pedigree, you grew up on a farm"

Gamble Beaurex:

"Your pussy is too dry to ride me this hard"

Sonja Morgan:

"OK, so I had a walk of shame. I admit it, I
Live for the walk of shame. Actually, I call it a
victory lap at my age!"

Tanya Bardsley:

"I'd eat donkey poo if it made me look younger."

Lisa Oldfield:

"She's old, she's a bitch and she deserves to be alone because she is a bitch."

Gina Liano:

"You're an insignificant ass hair!"

Andrea Moss:

"You were late, you left makeup all over my bathroom, you wore stilettos all over my $40,000 synthetic tennis court. You obviously don't have a tennis court. I do."

Kim Richards:

"Why don't you have a piece of bread and calm down a little"

Danielle Staub:

"Name change, I got arrested, pay attention please"

Monique Samuels:

"I'll drag you pregnant and all."

Bethenny Frankel:

"I need to start drinking alcohol, give me one of those bottles, get me some ice!"

Kenya Moore:

"Everyday, someone thinks I am Beyonce."

Ramona Singer:

"You were topless, you had sex on a waterbed, you kissed another woman, and you know what I never mentioned it, but if you want to mention it now we'll mention it."

Bethenny Frankel:

"MENTION IT ALL."

Porsha Williams:

"Girl them titties is aged hens, they're social distancing don't come for me."

Phaedra Parks:

"And she spends her weekends paddling through sperm banks looking through catalogues to try to find a donor. Honey you won't know if your baby daddy will be an axe murderer or a child molestor but what you will know is that he needed $10 for a medium sized pizza so he ejaculated in a cup so you could have a kid. Now check that."

Sonja Morgan:

"Maybe we are white trash but who cares, don't call me that."

Katie Rost:

"I'm sorry if I said you were dumb, maybe I meant that you were stupid."

Ashley Darby:

"You need to fill the void between your heart, not between your legs, girl."

Tamra Judge:

"Does your asshole get jealous of all the shit coming out your mouth?"

Kyle Richards:

"I thought I had a stroke but it was my false eyelashes making one eye smaller than the other."

Kathy Hilton:

"Who is Hunky Dory?"

Lisa Rinna:

"Let's talk about your arrest."

Dorit Kemsley:

"This is a cheeky little gift since we've all seen your pretty little puss now."

Lisa Barlow:

"If I give you a Chanel necklace and you choke on it that's your problem not mine."

Mary Cosby:

"Why is your aunt getting her legs cut off at 60? It's probably because her diet was bad. Drink water."

Luann De Lessops:

"Goodnight from the lower level."

Karen Huger:

"Ashley, you know what makes you so cute?
You're irritating as fuck."

Katie Rost:

"Just because you weren't there doesn't mean
I said it behind your back."

Sonja Morgan:

"Then you die and catch some dick along the way."

Kenya Moore:

"Sheree is screaming at me and acting crazy
as if I sliced the air mattress that she's been
sleeping on for the last four years."

Dorinda Medley:

"Clip clip BITCH!"

Terence Webb:

"Thank you for purchasing my housewives quote book!"